STAYING
SAFE

Staying safe in

PLAYGROUNDS

Maribeth Boelts

W

FRANKLIN WATTS
NEW YORK•LONDON•SYDNEY

This edition first published in the UK in 1998 by
Franklin Watts
96 Leonard Street
London
EC2A 4RH

Picture credits: Cover background and pp. 12, 16, 19, 20 by Seth Dinnerman;
p. 4 by Ira Fox; p. 7 Jeffrey Myers/FPG International Corp.; p. 8 © Stephen Simpson/FPG International
Corp.; p. 11 by Michael Brandt; p. 15 by Carrie Ann Grippo.

A CIP catalogue record for this book is available from the British Library.

ISBN 0 7496 3268 2

Printed in the United States of America

Contents

Kevin and Jen   5

Is my playground safe?   6

Playing safe   9

Swings   10

Slides   13

Climbers and see-saws   14

Accidents can happen   17

Danger: strangers   18

Protecting yourself   21

Friends and fun   22

Useful words   23

Index   24

Kevin and Jen

Kevin unpacked the last box in his room.
"I've finished. How about you?"
he called to his sister Jen.
They were moving into their new home.

"Me too," she answered. "Let's go and look
at the playground we saw in the park."

Jen went to find her dad. "Kevin and I think
you need a break from all this hard work.
Let's go to the park!"

◀ Moving home means hard work,
but also new places to explore.

Is my playground safe?

Playgrounds are great places to have fun.
But they must be safe. Is yours safe?
Check this list to find out.

• What is on the ground under the **equipment**? Woodchips, sand, pebbles or rubber are fine. **Concrete** or **asphalt** are very hard and could hurt you if you fall.

• Don't use equipment that is broken or rusty. A grown-up will tell you what's safe.

• Is the playground clean? Look out for rubbish and broken glass.

Materials like woodchips make the ground less hard if you fall. ▶

Playing safe

Playing safe means following a few rules
so that you stay safe and can
enjoy the playground.

- Always make sure a grown-up is there
to watch you.
- Tell your parent where you will be
and when you will be back.
- Only go to the playground during the day.
- With your parent, find the best **route**
to the playground. Stick to that route.
A shortcut could be **dangerous**.

Always go the playground
or park with friends.

Swings

Swings are fun, but falling off one isn't.
Sit on the seat and hold on to the chains
or rope with both hands.

If a friend is swinging next to you,
don't grab each other's swing.
When you've finished,
let the swing stop before you get off.

When you walk near swings,
leave plenty of space between you
and anyone who is swinging.

Holding on with both hands
is the safest way to swing. ▶

Slides

There are straight slides, bumpy slides
and slides that go round in a circle.

Whichever you like best,
use the ladder to get to the top.
Don't climb up the slide.
When you get to the top, sit down and wait
until the slide is clear before going down.
Always slide down with your feet first.

At the bottom, move out of the way
to let the next person have a turn.

◀ Always sit when you go
down the slide.

Climbers and see-saws

If you're playing on a climber, be careful
not to crash into the other children.
Make sure the bars are not wet.
If they are, you could slip and fall.

Playing on a see-saw is best with a friend
the same size as you. Otherwise the see-saw
won't go up and down very easily.

Tell your friend when you want to stop.
Then together you can make sure the see-saw
is level with the ground before you get off.

The best trick of all is
the trick of learning to stay safe. ▶

Accidents can happen

If an accident happens in the playground
and someone is hurt, stay calm. It just
makes things worse if you start crying too.

Call to a grown-up or go for help.
If you are with friends,
send one of them for help
while you stay with the person who is hurt.

Don't try to move someone who is hurt.
If the person is bleeding, use a cloth or hand
to press the cut until help arrives.

◀ Try to stay calm if you hurt yourself
in the playground.

Danger: strangers

Strangers are people you don't know.
Some look nice, some look nasty.
Some might try to hurt you.
So never accept money, presents or a lift
from anyone you don't know.

If a stranger comes to the playground,
tell a grown-up at once. If he or she tries
to talk to you, walk away. If you are scared,
go home and tell your parent.

It could be dangerous to talk to someone
you don't know, even if he or she looks nice. ▶

Protecting yourself

Here are ways you can **protect** yourself:
• Always go to the playground with another person.
• Don't accept sweets, money or a lift from anyone unless your parent says it's okay.
• If a stranger tries to talk to you, walk away.
• Your body belongs to you.
If someone tries to touch you in a way that makes you **uncomfortable**, say "No!" in a loud voice. Then run to a grown-up that you know and trust.

◀ Tell a grown-up if someone you don't know makes you feel nervous, scared or uncomfortable.

Friends and fun

Playgrounds are good places to make
new friends. If you've just moved home,
do what Kevin and Jen did at the beginning
of this book: go to the playground.

Running around and playing with friends
is good fun. It is also good exercise.

Exercise helps to keep you **healthy**.
That's another good reason
to go and have fun in the playground!

Useful words

Asphalt A thick, dark-coloured material used as a surface on roads and playgrounds.

Concrete A very hard material made of cement, sand, water and gravel.

Dangerous Something that can cause harm.

Equipment The swings, slides and climbers found in a playground.

Healthy Good for your body and mind.

Protect To keep from harm.

Route The path you take to get somewhere.

Stranger Someone you don't know.

Uncomfortable Feeling scared or unsure of yourself.

Index

A

accidents 17
asphalt 6

B

bleeding 17

C

calm, staying 17
climbers 14
concrete 6

E

exercise 22

F

friends 9, 10, 14, 17, 22

G

getting help 17, 18, 21
grown-ups 6, 9, 17, 18, 21

H

healthy, keeping 22

P

parent 9, 18, 21

protecting yourself 21

R

routes 9

S

safety 6, 9, 14
see-saws, 14
slides 13
strangers 18, 21
swings 10

U

uncomfortable, feeling 21